OUTLAWS AND LAWMEN
· OF THE WILD WEST ·

BUTCH
CASSIDY

REVISED EDITION

WANTED
DEAD OR ALIVE

By Carl R. Green and William R. Sanford

Enslow Publishers, Inc.
40 Industrial Road
Box 398
Berkeley Heights, NJ 07922
USA

http://www.enslow.com

Original edition published in 1995.

Library of Congress Cataloging-in-Publication Data
Green, Carl R.
  Butch Cassidy / by Carl R. Green and William R. Sanford. — Rev. ed.
      p. cm. — (Outlaws and lawmen of the wild West)
  Summary: "Readers will find out the truth and the myths surrounding the outlaw Butch Cassidy"—Provided by publisher.
  Includes bibliographical references and index.
  ISBN 978-0-7660-3175-3
  1. Cassidy, Butch, b. 1866—Juvenile literature. 2. Outlaws—West (U.S.)—Biography—Juvenile literature. 3. West (U.S.)—Biography—Juvenile literature. I. Sanford, William R. (William Reynolds), 1927– II. Title.
  F595.C362G743 2009
  364.15′5092—dc22
  [B]
                                          2008010007
ISBN-10: 0-7660-3175-6

Printed in the United States of America

10 9 8 7 6 5 4 3 2 1

To Our Readers:
We have done our best to make sure all Internet Addresses in this book were active and appropriate when we went to press. However, the authors and the publisher have no control over and assume no liability for the material available on those Internet sites or on other Web sites they may link to. Any comments or suggestions can be sent by e-mail to comments@enslow.com or to the address on the back cover.

♻ Enslow Publishers, Inc., is committed to printing our books on recycled paper. The paper in every book contains 10% to 30% post-consumer waste (PCW). The cover board on the outside of each book contains 100% PCW. Our goal is to do our part to help young people and the environment too!

Interior photos: The Art Archive/National Archives, Washington, DC, p. 43; Associated Press, p. 25; The Bridgeman Art Library, p. 19; Courtesy of butchandsundance.com, pp. 16, 26, 44 (right); Corbis/Jonathan Blair, pp. 7, 33; Corbis/Bettmann, pp. 9, 32, 34–35; iStockphoto/spxChrome, (marshal badge), odd pages; iStockphoto/Alex Bramwell (revolver), even pages; iStockphoto/billnoll (frame), pp. 4, 24, 36; Landov/Tyler Bridges/MCT, p. 40; Legends of America, pp. 1, 12, 21, 24, 28; Shutterstock/Dhoxax (background), pp. 3, 5, 10–11, 14–15, 18–19, 22–23, 27, 31, 36–37, 41; SuperStock/age footstock, p. 11; Telluride Historical Museum, pp. 14, 15; Utah State Historical Society, pp. 5, 36, 44 (left); Courtesy of Dobson/www.wyomingtalesandtrails.com, pp. 22, 30, 38; XNR Productions, p. 23.

Cover photo: Legends of America (*Butch Cassidy was photographed in 1894 during his only prison sentence. He served eighteen months for stealing horses.*)

TABLE OF CONTENTS

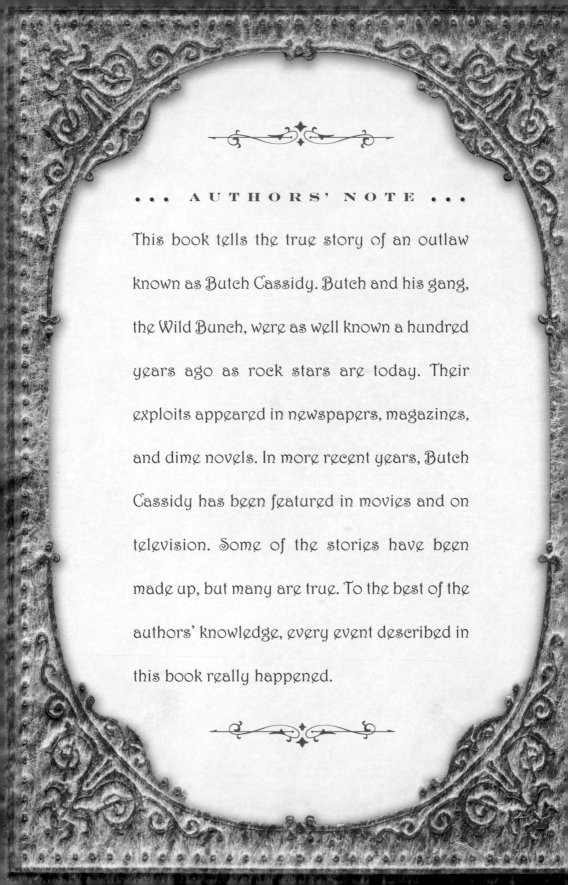

... AUTHORS' NOTE ...

This book tells the true story of an outlaw known as Butch Cassidy. Butch and his gang, the Wild Bunch, were as well known a hundred years ago as rock stars are today. Their exploits appeared in newspapers, magazines, and dime novels. In more recent years, Butch Cassidy has been featured in movies and on television. Some of the stories have been made up, but many are true. To the best of the authors' knowledge, every event described in this book really happened.

CHAPTER ONE

A SHOOT-OUT IN BOLIVIA

ometime around 1901, the daring western outlaw Butch Cassidy dropped out of sight. Americans were left to wonder about his fate. Almost thirty years later *The Washington Post* printed what seemed to be a final answer. "BUTCH IS DEAD" a headline screamed.

The news story was based on a 1930 magazine article. Arthur Chapman, writing in *Elks Magazine*, retold the story of Cassidy's life. Butch, Chapman wrote, had been a western Robin Hood. Beginning in

The famous outlaw Butch Cassidy was born Robert LeRoy Parker in 1866.

the late 1880s, Cassidy and his gang stole from rich cattle barons, bankers, and railroad tycoons. Chapman told his readers that after each robbery, the outlaws vanished into a Wyoming hideout known as Hole-in-the-Wall.

By 1900, the Wild West was coming to an end. Law and order were closing in on gunmen like Butch Cassidy. South America began to look like a safe haven for outlaws. Butch, the Sundance Kid, and Etta Place (Sundance's girlfriend) bought a ranch in Argentina. From 1902 to 1906, they worked the ranch and stayed out of trouble.

Their attempts to go straight ended in 1906. With the law closing in, the three friends turned again to crime. They robbed banks and mines in Argentina and Bolivia. Then Etta fell ill and returned to the United States.

Chapman reported that Butch and Sundance's luck ran out in 1909. A troop of Bolivian soldiers caught up with *Los Bandidos Yanquis* (the Yankee bandits). The troop's captain drew his pistol and entered the house where the outlaws were eating. "Surrender, *señores*," he cried. Instead of raising his hands, Butch grabbed his gun. His quick shot killed the captain.

The Sundance Kid and his girlfriend, Etta Place, pose for a formal portrait. Sundance's real name was Harry Longabaugh.

The soldiers stationed outside opened fire. Rifle bullets peppered the house's adobe walls. The outlaws, armed only with pistols, were badly outgunned. Sundance told Butch, "Keep me covered. I'll get our rifles." A moment later, Sundance was sprinting across the courtyard, firing as he ran. A bullet spun him around and he fell, badly wounded.

Butch risked his own life to drag his friend back to the house. By then, he was bleeding from several wounds. His cartridge belt was almost empty. Each time he tried to reach the rifles, the soldiers drove him back. At last darkness fell.

At about ten o'clock, the soldiers heard two shots. Then there was nothing but silence. Was it a trick? The long night crept past. At midday, the soldiers rushed the house, and found two bodies. As Chapman tells it, Butch had ended his friend's suffering with one shot. Then he used his last bullet on himself.

At last, it seemed, the mystery of Butch Cassidy's disappearance had been solved. His death in a bloody shoot-out satisfied the public's sense of right and wrong. Butch had lived by the gun and he had died by the gun.

Butch Cassidy, however, refused to stay buried. There were those who questioned Chapman's facts. Old friends and family members claimed they had

The 1969 film *Butch Cassidy and the Sundance Kid* was a Hollywood hit that revived the legend of these famous outlaws. Paul Newman (left) played Butch Cassidy. Robert Redford (right) played the Sundance Kid.

talked to the "dead" man. Butch had outfoxed the soldiers, they said. After returning home, he had taken a new name and built a new life.

In 1969, Hollywood revived the debate. In the hit film *Butch Cassidy and the Sundance Kid*, Paul Newman played Butch. Robert Redford took the role of Sundance. The movie ignored the reports that Butch had survived the shoot-out in Bolivia. The final scene shows Butch and Sundance dashing into a hail of rifle bullets.

Did Hollywood choose the wrong ending for its film? Read this story of the famous outlaw. Then make up your own mind.

... C H A P T E R   T W O ...

A MAVERICK GROWS UP

The year 1866 holds a special place in the story of the Wild West. In February, Jesse James robbed his first bank. On April 13, the baby who grew up to be Butch Cassidy was born in Beaver, Utah. Max (short for Maximillian) and Annie Gillies Parker named their firstborn Robert LeRoy Parker. They called him LeRoy, but most people knew him as Bob.

As a boy, Max Parker had sailed from England with his Mormon family. Iowa City was then the trailhead for the trek across the Great Plains. Faced with a shortage of wagons, the settlers loaded their goods onto two-wheeled handcarts. Then they pushed and pulled the carts 1,300 footsore miles to Utah.

When he grew up, Max married Annie Gillies in Beaver, Utah. The young husband found work carrying mail. Annie kept house and raised thirteen children. Bob grew up to be a sturdy, happy child. His younger

The future Butch Cassidy and his family settled near Circleville, Utah, in 1879. This was his home until 1884.

brothers and sisters looked up to him as their hero. To his mother's dismay, the fun-loving youngster resisted both schooling and religion.

In 1879, the Parkers bought a Circle Valley homestead. That winter the bitter cold killed most of their cattle. Thirteen-year-old Bob took a job on the nearby Marshall ranch. His pay helped feed and clothe the family. The ranch became Bob's school. He learned about horses, cattle, and good times from the cowboys.

The boy soon had his first brush with the law. One day he made the long ride into Circleville, only to find that the general store was closed. Instead of turning back,

In Utah and all over the West in the late 1800s, cattle roundups were a common sight. Young Bob Parker sometimes helped his friends round up cattle that actually belonged to the area's ranchers.

he broke into the store. Once inside, he calmly picked out a pair of jeans. As promise of payment, he dropped an IOU on the counter. The break-in angered the shopkeeper, who swore out a complaint. The matter was settled out of court, but Bob was learning to distrust the law.

At eighteen, Bob Parker stood five feet, nine inches tall and weighed 155 pounds. He had a quick, warm smile and a good sense of humor. His best friend was a skilled horse and cattle rustler named Mike Cassidy.

Mike put Bob through a crash course in riding, shooting, and rustling. Pleased by the teenager's progress, he gave his prize pupil a pistol and saddle. Annie Parker saw the danger and tried to pry her son away from Mike. She failed. Later, when he needed an alias, Bob "borrowed" Mike's last name.

In the 1880s, vast herds of cattle that belonged to wealthy ranchers roamed the region. For much of the year, no one tended the half-wild herds. To build up their own herds, struggling ranchers sometimes slipped in and rounded up young, unbranded cows. As proof of ownership, they marked these mavericks with their own brands.

In the spring of 1884, Bob went "mavericking" with some local ranchers, and the men gathered a good-sized herd. Back on the Marshall ranch they quickly branded their new livestock.

By June, some of the cattle had drifted back to their home range. Angry cattlemen took one look at the fresh brands and filed charges. The older ranchers talked young Bob into taking the blame. Over his mother's protests, he signed a paper saying he was the rustler. Then he saddled a fast horse and galloped out of town. Ahead lay Utah's badlands and its Robbers Roost hideout.

CHAPTER THREE

A BANK JOB AND A NEW NAME

For the next few years, Bob Parker dropped out of sight. That was easy to do in the lonely Robbers Roost country of southeast Utah. The trails he rode had never been mapped. Thanks to his skill with horses, he could always find work as a cowboy. When honest work grew tiresome, he stole horses and sold them. He still had a conscience, however. To protect his father's good name, he called himself George Cassidy.

Telluride, Colorado, was a fast-growing mining town in the 1880s.

In good times, he sent money home to his family.

Always restless, Bob moved on to southwest Colorado. Near the mining town of Telluride, he found

The Smuggler-Union Mine was one of the silver mines near Telluride. Bob Parker worked as a muleskinner, hauling ore from the mines.

work as a muleskinner. His mule teams hauled silver ore down to the mills in the San Miguel Valley. When he tired of hard work, Bob rode back to Robbers Roost. There he hooked up with a gang led by Bill and Tom McCarty. As a member of the McCarty gang, Bob became a regular on the owl-hoot trail. Until this time he had only flirted with the outlaw life.

In the spring of 1889, the gang ran short of cash. Bob told his new friends about the mine payrolls kept in Telluride's bank. With Tom McCarty and Matt Warner beside him, he returned to Telluride. By day, the three men studied the San Miguel Valley Bank. At night they drank and gambled in the town's saloons.

By the morning of June 24, the outlaws were ready. When they saw the cashier leave the bank, they moved in.

Tom held the horses and Bob guarded the door. Matt, dressed in a fine town suit, walked into the bank. He handed the teller a fake check, then pointed a gun at him. "Come on in, boys," he called. "It's all right."

Bob ran in, buckskin bags ready. He grabbed the money from the cash drawer and made a quick trip to the vault. When he left, the bags were bulging with $20,550. In 1889, this was a small fortune.

The robbers ran to their horses and galloped out of town. On Keystone Hill, Bert Charter was waiting with fresh mounts. Back in Telluride, Sheriff J. A. Beattie quickly called out a posse. One brave rider had already taken up the chase. He soon caught sight of the well-armed outlaws as they were changing horses. No fool, he stopped at the foot of Keystone Hill.

Bill McCarty led an outlaw gang with his brother Tom. Bob Parker joined the gang.

The posse soon caught up with the advance scout. The man pointed at the bank robbers, who were still switching saddles. When Charter spotted the danger, he acted quickly. First he tied a small fallen tree to the tail of one of the horses. Then he spooked the riderless horse and sent it galloping toward the posse. The tree scraped and bounced as the frightened horse bolted down the trail. The uproar panicked the posse's horses. By the time the lawmen regained control, the gang had vanished.

As soon as they reached their hideout, the outlaws divided up the loot. Then they went on a wild spree in the nearby towns. Bob liked whiskey, but the McCarty boys drank too much to suit him. He quit the gang and drifted from job to job.

One account says he picked up his nickname during this time. Drawn north to Wyoming, he found work in a Rock Springs meat market. The townsfolk liked the friendly young butcher. He gave honest service and kept candy in his pockets for the children. It seemed natural to call him Butch, a nickname often given to butchers.

Butch Cassidy was too footloose to stay tied to a town job. After leaving Rock Springs, he punched (herded) cows in the Brown's Hole region of northeast Utah. When spring came, he teamed up with Al Hainer. The partners bought a ranch on Horse Creek near Lander, Wyoming. The local paper reported that the men planned to raise fine horses. In town, their free-spending ways made friends quickly. The locals never guessed that Butch was living high on stolen money.

CHAPTER FOUR.

BUTCH CASSIDY'S LUCK TURNS SOUR

utch Cassidy and Al Hainer did not last long as horse breeders. They spent too much time in saloons and at Robbers Roost. Within the year, they sold the ranch and roamed more widely. Even so, they always had money in their jeans. This alerted the local cattle barons, since someone was stealing their horses and cattle. They kept a close watch on the two men.

One August day in 1891, Billy Nutcher appeared on the scene. Butch liked the looks of the three horses Nutcher was leading. The man was a known horse thief, but he swore these horses were his. Butch bought the story—and the horses. The matter might have ended there, but for rancher Otto Franc.

On August 28, Franc swore out a complaint. Butch and Al Hainer, he claimed, were riding stolen horses. Staying one jump ahead of the law, Butch and Hainer

Butch tried a career as a horse breeder, but soon turned back to crime. He was put on trial and jailed for stealing horses.

hid near Auburn, Wyoming. At last, in April 1892, Deputy Sheriff Bob Calverly caught up with them.

Calverly and a second lawman found Butch dozing on a cot. Calverly later wrote: "I told [Butch] I had a warrant for him and he said: 'Well, get to shooting,' and with that we both pulled our guns." In the struggle that followed, Butch's shot went wild. Calverly's first three shots missed, too. A fourth bullet grazed Butch's scalp, stunning him. Hainer gave up without a fight. The deputy handcuffed his prisoners and took them to jail.

On July 30, the partners were freed on $400 bail. Trial was delayed another ten months so that two key witnesses could testify. On June 20, 1893, in a district court at Lander, Butch's lawyer asked for a further delay. This time it was two of his witnesses who could not be found. The judge refused the request. Despite that setback, the trial went well for the defense. The men on the jury liked Butch. They found him not guilty.

Despite the acquittal, Butch's ordeal was not over. Otto Franc had filed a second complaint. This time he charged Butch with stealing the second of the three Nutcher horses. After making bail, Butch and Hainer parted ways. Friends had convinced Butch that his partner was working for Franc.

The second case came to trial in July 1894. A new jury convicted Butch of horse stealing, but set Hainer free. Butch most likely knew he was buying stolen stock, but he did not feel guilty. Franc, he believed, had set up the sale to trap him. On July 10, the judge sentenced Butch to two years of hard labor. In those days, that was a light sentence. Many horse thieves ended up hanging from the end of a rope. Some old-timers say that Butch left a sweetheart behind when he went to prison. If so, she may have been Mary Boyd, the pretty daughter of a pioneer settler. In later years, Mary claimed she had lived with Butch as his "common-law wife."

Convicted of stealing horses, Butch spent eighteen months in the Wyoming Territorial Prison in Laramie from 1894 to 1896.

Butch, who hated being locked up, learned to cope with prison life. He exercised in the prison yard and made new friends. With his pocket money, he bought books, candy, and tobacco.

In all, Butch served eighteen months in the Laramie prison. Legend has it that he won early release by making a pledge to the governor. "If you will pardon me," Butch said, "I will promise to leave the state of Wyoming alone." Trusting Cassidy to keep his word, Governor William A. Richards signed the papers.

On January 19, 1896, Butch left prison a free man. He was also a hard and bitter man. Prison, he claimed later, had truly turned him into an outlaw.

THE WILD BUNCH

A cabin at Hole-in-the-Wall in Wyoming was one of Butch's favorite hideouts.

Fresh from prison, Butch Cassidy looked for work as a cowhand. No one would hire him. His past hung over him like a dark cloud.

Butch shrugged and returned to the owl-hoot trail. It was time, he decided, to go for the big money—banks, trains, and payrolls. That meant he would need a tough gang beside him. To ensure the gang's safety, he would also need secure hiding places.

By this time Butch carried a map of good hideouts in his head. For his northern headquarters he chose Hole-in-the-Wall in central Wyoming. The Red Wall, a steep cliff fifty miles in length, sheltered this lush valley. Rolling a boulder into place would hide the single game trail into the valley.

Brown's Hole, near the Colorado-Wyoming border, served as a second hideout. Butch and his friend Elzy Lay built a cabin there. They picked a high rocky site now known as Cassidy's Point. Choosing a third safe haven was easy. Ever since he was young, Butch had been riding the Robbers Roost country of southeast Utah.

By ones and twos, a band of gunmen responded to Butch's call. The gang, he told them, would be called "the Train Robbers Syndicate." The newspapers of the day soon invented a more colorful name. Headline writers made the gang famous as "The Wild Bunch."

The Wild Bunch's crimes were spread over a large area. This made it harder for the law to catch up with the gang.

Butch's friend William Ellsworth "Elzy" Lay was an expert horseman and gunman. Unlike Butch, who never married, Lay and his wife raised two daughters. Butch called him "the educated member" of the group. He counted on Lay to plan the gang's train and bank robberies.

William Ellsworth "Elzy" Lay was Butch's friend and an important member of the Wild Bunch.

Harry Longabaugh was a second mainstay of the Wild Bunch. At seventeen, he had spent time in the Sundance, Wyoming, jail. Afterward, everyone took to calling him the Sundance Kid. Sundance was slow to smile, dressed like a dandy, and liked his liquor. His foes knew he was a crack shot. Butch worried that Sundance was too quick on the trigger.

The Wild Bunch attracted more than its share of top guns. Harvey Logan, better known as Kid Curry, was short, dark, and deadly. The quick-tempered Curry was second-in-command. Butch praised him as "the bravest man I ever knew." Henry "Bob" Meeks shared Butch's Mormon background. The two men had met while working as muleskinners. Ben Kilpatrick, a

The Wild Bunch (left to right): The Sundance Kid (Harry Longabaugh), Quiet Bill Carver, the Tall Texan (Ben Kilpatrick), Kid Curry (Harvey Logan), and Butch Cassidy (Robert Parker).

six-footer and a quick-draw expert, was called the Tall Texan. Despite a disfigured left eye, he was popular with the ladies. Quiet Bill Carver also came from Texas. The gang never let him forget the day he fought a losing battle with a skunk.

That summer the gang heard that Matt Warner was in jail. To raise cash to pay for his friend's lawyer, Butch decided to rob a bank. The bank in Montpelier, Idaho, looked like a good bet. The town's location,

Henry "Bob" Meeks knew Butch from their muleskinning days. He became a member of the Wild Bunch.

he saw, offered an easy escape route into Wyoming. Butch took a job on a nearby ranch while he scouted the bank.

On August 13, 1896, three men hit the bank at closing time. Meeks held the horses while Butch and Lay slipped inside. Lay held the bank clerks at gunpoint while Butch scooped up the money. Moments later, the two walked out with $6,615 in greenbacks and $1,000 in gold. As the outlaws raced out of town, a posse saddled up and rode in pursuit. That was when careful planning paid off. A fourth gang member was waiting with fresh mounts at Montpelier Pass. With their horses tiring, the posse gave up the chase.

Matt Warner's well-paid lawyer lost the case. After the trial, Butch offered to break his friend out of jail. Warner refused. He did not want to risk being shot in a jailbreak.

CHAPTER SIX

A SNOWFALL OF GREENBACKS

he Wild Bunch pulled only a few jobs a year. The months between holdups gave the gang time to relax. Also, Butch Cassidy needed time to plan each robbery. In the spring of 1897, he decided to specialize in trains and payrolls.

On April 21, the Denver & Rio Grande chugged into Castle Gate, Utah. Paymaster E. L. Carpenter was on hand to pick up the Pleasant Valley Coal Company payroll. Butch and Elzy Lay had waited a week for this moment. As Carpenter and his aides walked past, Butch stepped forward. He jammed his pistol into the paymaster's ribs and grabbed the payroll satchel. Lay took a smaller bag from one of the aides. Moments later, the outlaws were raising dust as they galloped out of town.

Carpenter gathered a small posse and ran to the waiting train. Uncoupled from its cars, the engine was soon whizzing down Pine Canyon gorge. No one saw

Butch and Lay, hidden behind a shed while they changed horses. From there, the outlaws turned south, leaving two posses fanning out to the north. Three changes of horses later, the two men circled back toward Brown's Hole.

The gang soon spent most of the $8,800 payroll on good times. Townsfolk welcomed the Wild Bunch at times like these. No one complained if Butch and the boys shot up the place. They paid saloonkeepers a dollar for every bullet hole they left in a bar.

Less than two months later, the Wild Bunch hit another bank. This time the target was Belle Fourche, South Dakota. Some accounts say that Butch rode with the gang that day. Others insist that Kid Curry was in charge. Only one fact is certain. The Wild Bunch could not have pulled off all the jobs charged to their account.

The Wild Bunch spent some of its stolen money in saloons like this one in Colorado.

After Belle Fourche, the gang took a two-year break. The men had plenty of cash and the law was closing in. In 1898, some of them joined the army and fought in the Spanish-American War. Butch and Lay hired on at the WS Ranch in Alma, New Mexico. Butch introduced himself as Jim Lowe. The manager liked the way he handled cattle and made him foreman. Teamed with Lay, Butch kept the ranch running smoothly.

The holiday from crime ended in June 1899. The war was over, and the gang was coming together again. Butch set his sights on a new target.

At 2:18 A.M. on June 2, the Overland Flyer was heading toward Wilcox, Wyoming. Engineer W. R. Jones braked the train when he saw a red lantern ahead. As the engine slid to a stop, two masked men stepped out of the darkness. They forced the crew to uncouple the express car and engine. Then they ordered Jones to pull the express car across a nearby bridge. When the engineer was slow to obey, Kid Curry pistol-whipped him.

Four more masked men ran up and hammered on the express car. The frightened clerk refused to open the door. The outlaws solved the problem by blowing the door off with dynamite. After the smoke cleared, they rolled the unconscious clerk out of the car. Then they dynamited the safe. The blast blew wads of

The Overland Flyer's express car was where the train's safe was located. To get to the money, gang members blew up the car and the safe with dynamite.

paper money skyward. Soon it seemed to be snowing greenbacks. Sticky reddish drops stained some of the bills. The "blood" turned out to be juice from a crate of raspberries. As the dust settled, the outlaws took more than $30,000 from the shattered safe.

Heavy rain bogged down the gang's getaway. Even though the outlaws changed horses three times, a posse tracked and cornered them. In the shootout that followed, Kid Curry killed Sheriff Joe Hazen. With their leader dead, the other lawmen broke off the chase.

Was Butch Cassidy one of the masked men? If so, he broke the hands-off-Wyoming pledge he had made three years before. Even if he was not there, he most likely planned the job. Either way, his picture went up on wanted posters throughout the region.

CHAPTER SEVEN

ONE STEP AHEAD OF THE LAW

The Wild Bunch struck again on July 11, 1899. Butch Cassidy may have planned the job, but Elzy Lay and Kid Curry carried it out. The outlaws stopped a train near Folsom, New Mexico, and made off with $30,000. A posse surprised the fleeing gang members at Turkey Creek. Three lawmen were killed in the firefight that followed and Lay was badly wounded. He managed to escape, only to be captured that fall and sent to prison.

Law and order were becoming the new spirit of the West. The Union Pacific hired the Pinkerton National Detective Agency to catch the Wilcox train robbers. One by one, lawmen and detectives found the gang's hideouts. Posses made use of the railroads, the telephone, and the telegraph to cut off escape routes. Fast horses no longer guaranteed safety.

The Union Pacific Railroad put together a "super posse" to catch the thieves who stole $45,000 from one of its trains.

Butch spent the winter of 1899 in Texas. Perhaps he was tiring of being hunted. He hired a Salt Lake lawyer to ask for amnesty. The governor of Utah turned him down, but the lawyer had better luck with the railroad. Drop all charges, he said, and Butch Cassidy will go straight. A meeting was arranged, but a storm delayed the railroad officials. When they failed to appear, Butch was certain he had been double-crossed.

On August 29, 1900, the Wild Bunch stopped a Union Pacific train outside Tipton, Wyoming. Cassidy was not there, but Kid Curry was. Because the train was stopped on an incline, Curry allowed the crew to set the brakes on the passenger cars. Then he ordered the engineer to pull the express and mail cars to a safe distance. After blowing up the safe with three charges of dynamite, the outlaws vanished. The railroad announced that the raid had netted only $50.40. Butch laughed when he heard the report. The gang had ridden off with a cool $45,000, he later wrote. The express car clerk backed his claim.

Kid Curry led the holdup of the Union Pacific train near Tipton, Wyoming, in 1900.

The railroads fought back by offering rewards. They also put some of the West's best marksmen and trackers on a special train. Each man carried field glasses and a high-powered rifle. The train was equipped with a loading ramp, horse stalls, and a fast engine. It stood on a track in Wyoming, ready to go.

Butch did not want to tangle with the super posse. For his next target he chose a town far to the west. On September 19, Butch, Sundance, and Bill Carver hit the bank at Winnemucca, Nevada. The bank president took one look at their pistols and opened the vault. The outlaws stuffed $32,640 into sacks and herded five hostages out the back door. Then they mounted their horses and rode out of town, guns blazing. Carver almost spoiled the getaway. He dropped a bag of gold coins and foolishly stopped to retrieve it.

A telephone call sent lawmen from the next town in hot pursuit. The chase lasted for days, but the gang members were riding faster horses. After the posse turned back, the outlaws headed to Fort Worth, Texas. The five men felt safe there and had a good time spending the bank's money. They bought stylish suits and even posed for a group

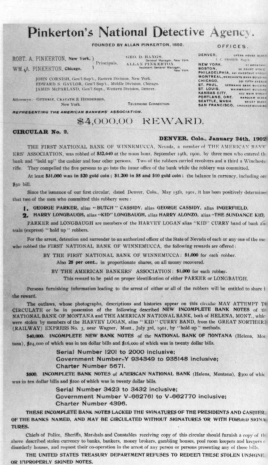

The Pinkerton National Detective Agency issued this poster describing Butch, Sundance, and other members of the Wild Bunch after the bank robbery in Nevada. It offered a $4,000 reward for their capture.

photo. As a joke, Butch sent a copy to Winnemucca. His note thanked the bank for its donation.

On July 3, 1901, the Great Northern Coast Flyer stopped for water near Wagner, Montana. Kid Curry jumped aboard. After crawling over the coal tender, he took command of the engine. A volley of warning shots sent passengers ducking back into the cars. Once again, the express car was uncoupled and pulled up the track. Once again, a dynamite blast cracked the safe. The outlaws were $65,000 richer when they rode away.

Butch knew it was time to break up the Wild Bunch. After they outrode the pursuit, the men shook hands. Then, two by two, they rode off to start new lives.

CHAPTER EIGHT

LOS BANDIDOS YANQUIS

Butch Cassidy had heard that Argentina did not extradite American outlaws. That vast country, with its growing cattle industry, looked like a perfect refuge. Sundance agreed to go with him. Their long trip began with a stop in New York City. Like tourists everywhere, they spent their days enjoying the sights of the big city.

Sundance took Etta Place with him. Some sources say she was a Denver schoolteacher. Others say she met Sundance while working in a Texas "sporting house." In *The Outlaw Trail,*

Etta Place could ride and shoot just as well as most men of that time.

Robert Redford calls her the granddaughter of an English lord. Whatever her background, Etta was never a burden. Brave, green-eyed, and a crack shot, she rode as well as most of the men.

Sundance and Etta sailed for Argentina in February 1902. To confuse the Pinkertons, Butch left by way of Canada. From there he caught a ship bound for England. At Liverpool, he boarded a cattle boat headed for South America.

In April 1902, the three fugitives met in Buenos Aires. They put $12,000 in a bank account and bought land in southern Argentina. The remote ranch at Chubut was soon stocked with sheep, cattle, and horses. Butch and Sundance enjoyed their new role as gentlemen ranchers. Etta served as hostess. When she helped work the ranch, she often pulled on riding pants and rode bareback.

For four years, the trio lived a peaceful life. Butch even urged friends back home to join him. In the eyes of the law, however, he was still a wanted man. In 1906, an American cattle buyer recognized the fugitives. Eager to collect a reward, the man asked the local police to make an arrest. The law moved slowly in that part of the world, however. Forewarned, Butch and Sundance had time to sell the ranch before they moved northward.

Once they reached Argentina in 1902, Butch, Sundance, and Etta Place met up in Buenos Aires (above). Then they moved on to a remote ranch in the southern part of the country.

Butch had guessed wrong about finding a safe refuge in Argentina. He guessed right when he said that South America was ripe for plucking. During the next year, he and Sundance touched off a minor crime wave. With Etta holding the horses, they robbed four banks, two express trains, and four pack trains. Etta rode side by side with the men until illness forced her to return to the United States. Her outlaw days were over.

The region buzzed with stories of *Los Bandidos Yanquis*. A few of the jobs produced big payoffs. In Rio Galleos, a bank vault yielded $20,000. When on the run, the outlaws often hid in Indian villages. Gifts of gold and candy bought food, lodging, and safety. The Indians kept a stony silence when questioned by the police.

The partners found honest work between holdups. In the spring of 1907, Butch took a job at the Concordia Tin Mines in Bolivia. He called himself Jim Maxwell. A week later, the mine hired Sundance, who signed on as Enrique Brown. From time to time, the two men rode off to hijack mine payrolls. In 1908, manager Clement Glass learned their real names. Holding them at gunpoint, he warned them not to rob his mine. Butch and Sundance told him not to worry. They never stole from their friends, they said.

Mine official Percy Seibert became one of those friends. He and his wife shared Sunday meals with the outlaws. One night in 1909, Butch said, "I guess it's time to pull out." Seibert could see that his friend was looking older than his years. Soon afterward, *Los Bandidos* held up another mule train. As part of his loot, Butch helped himself to a fine silver-gray mule.

San Vicente is a small town in southern Bolivia. Many people believe that Butch and Sundance died there in 1909.

Days later, at San Vicente, a constable spotted the mule. Knowing he was outgunned, he called in a troop of cavalry.

The gunfight that ends the film *Butch Cassidy and the Sundance Kid* followed. The soldiers seemed certain that the dead men were Butch and Sundance. Seibert, who knew the men well, confirmed their deaths.

The news slowly made its way north to the United States. The leaders of the Wild Bunch, it seemed, had died with their boots on.

CHAPTER NINE

DEAD OR ALIVE?

Dead outlaws do not come back to life. Even so, many people swear that Butch Cassidy did return from Bolivia. This "new" Butch Cassidy, they tell us, called himself William T. Phillips. As Phillips, he married, built a business, and raised a child.

Let's look at the facts we do have. Lula Parker Betenson tells her version in *Butch Cassidy, My Brother*. Arthur Chapman's story of Butch's death was more fiction than fact, she insisted. In her book, Betenson describes a 1925 visit with her brother in great detail.

How does the "Butch-didn't-die" crowd explain Percy Seibert's role? They insist that Seibert lied to Arthur Chapman. He may have wanted the world to think his friend was dead. Given a fresh start, Butch would be free to build a new life. Researchers have found that the Bolivian Army has no record of the San Vicente gunfight. Western author Larry Pointer did his best to dig up the truth. His research convinced him that William Phillips really was Butch Cassidy.

According to Pointer, Phillips first appeared in Adrian, Michigan, in the spring of 1908. That was the year *before* Butch Cassidy's reported death. He told his neighbors that he owned a machine shop in Iowa. Within a few weeks, he met, courted, and married Gertrude Livesay.

The couple soon headed south to Arizona. The desert climate, they hoped, would help Gertrude's asthma. Phillips later claimed that he rode as a sharpshooter with Pancho Villa during this time. The Mexican bandit chief paid him six dollars a day, Phillips said. Two years later, the couple moved to Spokane, Washington. Along the way they paid a visit to Hole-in-the-Wall.

In Spokane, Phillips worked as a draftsman. He also went prospecting for gold in Alaska. There he met Wyatt Earp, the great lawman. Earp later said he was certain the man called Phillips was really Butch Cassidy. Back in Spokane, Phillips invented an adding machine and started the Phillips Manufacturing Company. In 1919, William and Gertrude adopted a baby boy. In 1925, the family moved to a fine large home. Times were good.

That same summer, Phillips told his wife that he was going to South America on business. The lie freed him to revisit his past. After looking up old friends in Wyoming, he drove to his family home in Utah. Forty-one years had passed since he left. Max Parker was eighty-one, but the old man was certain this man was his son.

Phillips's business failed in 1930. From 1933 on, he worked at odd jobs. In his spare time, he wrote his version of Butch Cassidy's life. He put his heart into *The Bandit Invincible*, but no one would publish the badly-written book. At one

Even Wyatt Earp, the great lawman, was convinced that William Phillips was Butch Cassidy.

low point in 1935, Phillips thought of returning to crime. His plot to kidnap a wealthy Spokane man never went past the planning stage, however. By that time, Phillips was an ailing sixty-nine. Riddled with cancer, he died at the county poor farm in 1937.

Could William Phillips have been Butch Cassidy? *The Bandit Invincible* contains details that only Butch

Robert LeRoy Parker, also known as Butch Cassidy, appears on the left. William T. Phillips is pictured on the right. Are they the same person? What do you think?

could have known. A handwriting expert compared letters written by the two men. The expert felt certain the same hand produced both letters. Challenging that proof is the hard fact that Phillips surfaced in Michigan at least six months before the shootout in Bolivia.

Whatever the truth of Phillips's claims, Butch Cassidy's legend lives on. The reasons are easy to understand. Most western outlaws were grim, deadly killers. Butch was a sunny, bighearted man. Although he robbed banks and trains, he never stole from the poor. He also avoided gunplay whenever he could. Forget William Phillips, his fans say. Load up the DVD player and watch Butch go out in a final blaze of rifle fire. That's the stuff of which legends are made.

GLOSSARY

adobe—Sun-dried bricks made of clay and straw. A building made of these bricks is also called an adobe.

alias—An assumed name. Western outlaws often used aliases to conceal their true identities.

amnesty—A legal document that forgives suspected criminals for any offenses they may have committed.

bail—Money paid to a court to guarantee the return of a suspect for trial.

cattle barons—A reference to the owners of large cattle ranches in the Wild West. Because of their power and wealth, these owners sometimes ruled their lands like medieval lords.

common-law wife—In the Wild West, men and women sometimes set up housekeeping without going through a marriage ceremony. After the couple lived together as if husband and wife for a time, the woman gained a legal status known as common-law wife.

complaint—A legal claim in which one citizen charges another with a financial or physical injury.

constable—A low-ranking lawman who keeps the peace in a town or village.

dime novels—Popular fiction printed in low-cost books and magazines during the late 1800s.

express car—A special baggage car equipped to carry a train's cargo of mail, gold, cash, and other valuables.

extradite—To return accused criminals to the state or country in which they will stand trial.

greenbacks—A slang term for U.S. paper money.

handcarts—Small two-wheeled carts on which Mormon settlers carried their household goods across the Great Plains.

"IOU"—A promise to pay a debt. The initials stand for "I owe you."

jury—A group of citizens sworn to judge the facts and reach a verdict in a court case.

legend—A story that many people believe but which is often untrue in whole or in part.

mavericks—In the Wild West, unbranded calves who were found roaming free. Tradition said that mavericks belonged to the first person to brand them.

muleskinner—Anyone who drove a mule team in the Wild West. The name was taken from the long leather whip the muleskinner used to control the team.

owl-hoot trail—Wild West slang for choosing the life of an outlaw.

pistol-whipped—To be beaten with a pistol.

posse—A group of citizens who join with lawmen to help capture fleeing outlaws.

railroad tycoons—A reference to the rich and powerful men who owned the railroads of the Wild West.

rustler—An outlaw who steals horses or cattle.

Spanish-American War—The 1898 war between Spain and the United States.

sporting house—Wild West slang for a house of prostitution.

trailhead—The city or town from which travelers set off to follow a wilderness trail.

FURTHER READING

Books

Bard, Jessica. *Lawmen and Outlaws: The Wild, Wild West.* Danbury, Conn.: Children's Press, 2005.

Doeden, Matt. *The World's Most Notorious Crooks.* Mankato, Minn.: Capstone Press, 2007.

Rutter, Michael. *Wild Bunch Women: True Stories of the Feisty Females Who Traveled with Butch Cassidy and His Infamous Wild Bunch.* Guilford, Conn.: Globe Pequot Press, 2003.

Internet Addresses

Butch Cassidy and the Sundance Kid
http://www.wyomingtalesandtrails.com/butch.html

History of Butch Cassidy, LeRoy Parker
http://www.utah.com/oldwest/butch_cassidy.htm

The Wild West Cowboys & Legends: Butch Cassidy & The Sundance Kid
http://www.thewildwest.org/interface/index.php?action=275

INDEX